FEELINGS DRIVE BEHAVIOUR

Learn the Secret to Eliminating Your Child's Difficult Behaviour Quickly and Easily Without Discipline, Drugs or Therapy

BECS MCEWAN

REBECCA

You got me spinning around the eye of the hurricane
allowing me to take control,
Taking a swing at the emotions as they rise,
Riding them all the way down through the hole.
Years of pain, trauma and chaos, caught up in
this treacherous storm,
Facing each emotion completely head on
as they come out to perform.
I feel this heaviness in my chest, I just want
to let it go,
Overridden with fear, trapped in the memory,
sinking down to another low.
I feel like I'm out of control as my body starts to shake,
In the back of my mind, the doubt seeps in,
from this nightmare I want to wake.
The sound of your voice in the distance as I wade
through the darkness,
Allowing me to feel safe and secure as I battle the intensity
of the emotions.
I know this is just the beginning, it's going to take some time,
to battle this feisty hurricane, and drop down
through the eye of the storm.

Ashley Highnam

ABOUT THE AUTHOR

Becs McEwan is a Behaviour specialist, speaker, an entrepreneur and now the author of her first book.

Becs teaches children and their parents how to interrupt lifelong patterns of behaviour by helping them uncover the root cause, quickly and easily with her proven and very effective method and techniques.

Transforming lives instantly! Without the need for discipline, drugs or therapy.

Over the last 7 years Becs has facilitated miraculous change for hundreds of families globally and is currently developing an online platform so she can share her message on a larger scale.

Becs travels regularly to the United States to attend Business Masterminds with other leaders in their fields and believes in surrounding herself with like minded forward-thinking individuals!

In her spare time, she enjoys pushing the limits taking on new adventures skydiving, horse riding and rally driving through New Zealand bush, she encourages herself to be the best version of herself she can be.

But it has not always been this way. Becs spent much of her life depressed and anxious, repeating patterns of behaviour that were not healthy, nor did they serve her.

Now what drives her is to show others how to break their behaviour patterns, their habits and deconstruct their conditioned belief systems. Allowing them to unlock the pure potential that sits inside of them, mostly unnoticed and certainly underutilised, covered only by the learnt patterns of behaviour.

Since 2014 Becs McEwan has been providing her services to many Government Agencies, New Zealand's largest Intermediate school and the local police, as well as seeing private clients from her home-based clinic and providing site-based staff training for local businesses.

Becs originally from Scotland now lives with her partner in life and in business, Roger, and Becs teenage children, Cam and Jess.

It was her trailblazing nature that brought her to the distant shores of New Zealand in 2002, when Cameron was only 16 months old in search of a better life for her family. The path that was to unfold was certainly not the one she had planned, but it has been, like everything, perfect in its evolution.

With the insights and techniques Becs has uncovered combinded with the deep understanding she has gained from her clients and through her own personal experiences. Becs now teaches children and their parents how to Identify the conditioned response and Deactivate the incomplete emotional experience that sits at the root and is driving the behaviour .

ACKNOWLEDGMENTS

I am most grateful to my partner Roger Hardie who has stood by me and supported me wholeheartedly over the last 7 years. Holding me accountable in my quest to find my true self. He too has been committed to the process, tirelessly deactivating his own coding and reaching for new levels of immersion in the game of life. Regularly holding space for me to recognise my own conditioned patterns and limitations. Without him I believe I would still be in a marriage that was suffocating me, running a business that was killing me and stuck in patterns of behaviour that were destructive and damaging. He has always seen my light, and it has been with his unconditional love that I have been able to uncover it and shine it in the world.

Michael Stratford and Tom Stone for their contribution. Both played a large role in my early understanding of the human condition and the insights into the insidious nature of our childhood conditioning. Both men have deeply influenced my life in ways that cannot be expressed, I will be forever grateful for their contribution.

I am grateful to my family for the lessons and gifts they have brought and will continue to bring. You are all amazing and I love you. The unsung heroes behind this book, Caroline Veevers, John McCabe, Ed Rush, Mike Koenigs.

To my clients who have brought me to new levels of understanding not only of the work I facilitate, but also of myself. Many of you have become dear friends and have agreed to have your stories shared as part of this book. I am so grateful to you for having the courage to face your Truths and your Monsters to experience the powerful shifts that occur when you simply Identify and Deactivate your **Human Control Codes**. Without you none of this would have been possible.

For the individuals who sit deep within the 'systems', Educational, Justice and Government, those of you who have been open enough to explore other options for the children under your care. I am so grateful for you. Because of you I have been able to explore this new approach! You were all aware that the current ways of dealing with anxiety, depression and behavioural issues were not working and you were willing to try another way!

The Emotional Health of our world is in crisis.

You allowed me to share my method of Identifying and Deactivating incomplete emotional experiences to release the children from their emotional pain. Changing patterns of behavior that previously seemed impossible to change.

I believe that if we focus on our Emotional Health, there will be shifts that our minds have never have considered.

INTRODUCTION

A book about Feelings? So What?

Then, I realized that although it was such a simple concept; Feelings Drive Behaviour, the power of it was immense and life changing and available to everyone if they only knew where to look and what to do when they uncovered the underlying cause.

We have a society that has become very focused on labelling and assessing behaviours, then treating or managing their symptoms. As parents we love to; have a justified reason why for why our child is behaving so badly, if there is a recognised and 'legitimate' reason for it, if feels less like our fault.

Having spoken with hundreds of distraught parents and teachers over the years that is where the answers seemed to stop, the labels, the assessment. The What to do now? and How can we help the child? seems to be another story.

You can talk about it with a councillor or delve deeper into the definition of what and why, with a psychologist. They teach you coping mechanisms and strategies with behaviour therapies and parenting and anger management courses or you can medicate your child and mask the symptoms, and then learn to cope with the side effects.

The soul purpose of this book is I wanted you to understand one simple truth, underlying ALL behaviour patterns is an uncomfortable feeling that we are trying to avoid.

Feelings Drive Behaviour.

This book has the best of both worlds, intellectual understanding and client experiences.

What you find inside is the theory behind the behaviour patterns and an explanation of how they were put in place. I share stories from parents and individuals who have experienced my method and coaching programes and the life changing results they and their children have enjoyed. The method is based on proven techniques that I have been using with families and individuals over the years.

The results speak for themselves.

Check out becsmcewan.com for Free Resources.

One piece of advice: use the resources. They will help you to delve deeper into your child's behaviour patterns and how to Identify and Deactivate the underlying cause giving you and your child greater emotional freedom.

On that note, the difference between ordinary and extraordinary relationships comes down to implementation. The difference is your willingness to implement the things you learn.

The same is true for the information in this book. It works, and similar to everything you learn, it only works when implemented. You knowing all of this information won't help your child behave any better or you feel more relaxed and happy. However, when you implement, and consistently use the techniques you can help your child and have the relationship with your child that you want, PLUS you will feel happier and more relaxed and you will notice all the relationships in your life will be positively enhanced.

One of the most common questions I get from distraught parents is, "How am I supposed to get my kid to comply and engage with the process?"

The secret is that once you begin to understand what is driving your child's behaviour, you will very quickly see the illusion the Behaviour Patterns are playing out in your own life, too. Once you have this awareness and are able to start Identifying and Deactivating theses patterns of behaviour and conditioning for yourself, you will discover your childs behaviour patterns will no longer trigger you. You will also find space and calm in the relationship, often this is enough of a shift to alter the dynamics of your parent / child relationship and the Unwanted behaviours in your child simply fall away.

At becsmcewan.com we have included a section where you can find out how to work with me either in one of my Parent / Child workshops or through my individual coaching programmes.

But for now, let us get started.

TABLE OF CONTENTS

DID YOU EVER THINK PARENTING WOULD BE THIS HARD?

Do you dread what your child will do next, the next phone call from the school or the police?

Do you lie in bed at night feeling sick to your stomach at the thought of another day in the battle field your home has become?

Did you ever think that parenting would be this hard?

Do you long for a quiet and peaceful home?

Would you like to be able to talk and have your child listen?

What would it be like to have a child that is happy and shows you love and respect?

What would life be like without the stress?

Or maybe you are sick with worry because your child has developed a pattern of behaviour, a routine or a ritual that you both find distressing.

Nightmares and chronic irrational fears can become quite disruptive to the entire household.

I wrote this book to share with you the experience I had in curing myself of Anxiety and Unwanted Behaviour Patterns and how that has led me onto becoming a Behaviour Specialist and an Emotional Wellbeing Consultant!

The insights that I had into my *Adult Bad Behaviour*, stress and exhaustion, shouting at my kids, being reactive, argumentative and verbally aggressive towards my family, husband, and sometimes even the customers in my café. It was then that I recognised I was caught in patterns of behaviour, emotional breakdowns, depression and anxiety with regular suicidal thoughts, all learnt behavior patterns. Addiction to nicotine and pharmaceutical drugs and a marijuana habit that was becoming a daily occurance, I was always looking for a way to escape the emotional pain I was in, all of them where patterns of behaviour keeping me away from a feeling!

What I am going to share with you in this book helped me understand myself and my children in a whole new way.

Simply by understanding that the Patterns of Behaviour your child is displaying, are just that, patterns of subconscious conditioning, the source coding of which lies deep within their subconscious.

I will show you what it is that is really triggering and activating their difficult behaviour!

I can help you;

- Change the way you think and feel about yourself, and your child, all your relationships and your work and home environments.

- Transform the way you interact with your child to empower you to proactively seek the changes you have been afraid to make.

- Surrender the need to be a people pleaser and not be afraid that your child will stop loving you if you don't give in to their bad behaviour and tantrums.

- You will free yourself from the hurt and worry of what other's think of you and your child, you will stop feeling embarrassed and judged for your child's behaviour.

- Develop the confidence to handle difficult situations with ease.

- Reclaim a sense of purpose and passion for your life, as you are no longer caught in the exhausting energy generated by your child's behaviour.

- Discover self-acceptance and develop the ability to love all of who you are (and your child).

- Learn to embrace your own uniqueness and significance to others and help develop this ability in your child.

- Move beyond possibility into the realm of the unimaginable.

THE SECRET TO HAPPINESS

Bubbly, happy, positive and energetic is how most would remember me from school, friends and colleagues throughout my life time until I hit my early 30's when it became more and more difficult to 'Be Happy' It was a real effort sometimes to even put a smile on my face.

When I was born my parents were living in Kenya, East Africa. They were on the adventure of a lifetime, my mum in her early 20's accompanied my Dad who was teaching chemistry to the boys at Thika High School.

As a family of 4, we returned to Scotland in 1975 as the political platform in East Africa was shaky and my parents decided was not the most ideal environment to bring up a young family. Shortly after returning my father started teaching at Morrisons Academy, a private boarding school in central Scotland. I attended this school as a 'Day bug' from 4 years old till I turned 17, and I found it tough. I struggled academically, suffering with Dyslexia and I am sure I would have been labelled ADHD, has it been a 'thing' 40 years ago. I had never been particularly good at sport and didn't enjoy being part of a team. I was bullied at school and always felt like an outsider and somehow different.

I always felt trapped in a world that stifled my creativity and individuality.

My "black cloud" days started in my early teenage years and I turned to the usual ways of relieving my unhappiness. Drinking, recreational drug taking, partying, boyfriends and my favourite was to 'run away', travel to far off places!

By the time I was in my late 20's, my dark days had become more and more intense and frequent. I was living and working in Edinburgh. I was the office manager for a small trendy up and coming Architect firm and was preparing to launch a Design and Branding division to the business, I was on fire! (on the outside) I'd come home and crash!

I had met my soul mate, my 'forever and always' and we married in the Serengeti game reserve in Tanzania, Africa.

We loved to buy and renovate property and were lucky to flip a couple of properties in the Boom that Edinburgh experienced in the late 90's.

To all intense and purposes, we were 'Happy', making money, working hard, partying hard, life was good.

Then I found out I was pregnant!

I was terrified of being a parent, I had never really had the maternal urge and I was only just coping with things the way they were.

Not long after the birth of my son, I repeated a pattern of behaviour I used when I felt trapped, I changed location.

We sold our house, left our jobs, our friends and family and with a 16-month-old baby emigrated across the globe from Scotland to New Zealand. It was only years later I saw the irony in what I had done.

The pattern had been re-set.

I joined a fabulous family owned company where the career opportunities seemed endless, my colleagues became my family and friends and I was 'Happy', but for how long?

It didn't take long at all before the arrival of my black clouds, foreboding and threatening a storm.

A year after we had arrived in paradise I fell pregnant with my daughter and this time my wheels really fell off.

I was angry and upset as default now. My morning sickness was severe and prolonged lasting almost the whole pregnancy. I was heavily medicated with anti-depressants and after Jess was born I found it difficult to connect or bond with her, this compounded the hopelessness I was already feeling.

I was on uppers and downers, I started having debilitating migraines (more medication) bouts of vomiting that would last for days (prescribed pills and potions), my partner the love of my life was now my verbal and emotional punch bag. I stopped eating regularly and would binge on sugar and carbs. I was smoking 20- 30 cigarettes a day and would smoke 3 - 4 joints a day as well, and still mostly to the outside world I was 'Happy'. I had a big house, nice car, a husband, 2 kids, my own business, what more was there?

When I was admitted into hospital after a five day stretch of vomiting and headaches I weighed 42kg and despite all their best efforts (poking and prodding and more drugs) they were unable to find a cause.

By the tenth day I had given up my will to live, it was in that very same moment, that my life started to change.

I had hit rock bottom!

There was a SHIFT in my consciousness. An unexplainable experience!

I discharged myself from hospital and refused to continue with any of the pharmaceuticals. I was gentle with my body and my mind as I faced a period of convalescence. I read a lot of personal development books and became intrigued by the link between my body and my emotions.

I learnt about energy and the power of our intention and I started to heal myself from the inside out.

I did have a habit of running before I could walk. I found what I considered to be an amazing opportunity and started to create what I believed to be the perfect bussiness in the perfect location.

It wasn't long before I found myself stuck in another nightmare, one that I had created for myself and my family.

We had decided to open a beautiful Café in the woods. My husband and I had built the business from scratch using our life savings and loans from our parents, to create our dream. We had both taken a leap of faith, leaving our corporate jobs and stepping into the world of the self-employed, we became business owners.

I was the creative force and my husband was the business mind and together we built a business. Neither of us really had any idea how hard it would be or what toll it would have on our family life and our financials. Very quickly we found ourselves out of our depth.

I was out of my comfort zone on so many levels and I was in deep trouble, again, not only financially but emotionally.

I was out of control, I wanted the world to stop and let me get off. My emotional wellbeing was in chaos and my behaviour was reactive and manic I was anxious and suicidal all the time!

I was scared I would end up in hospital again, so I decided to take action.

THE WAY WE SEE THE WORLD

My first major shift was becoming aware that it was my way of seeing things, my perception that had me trapped inside a life that was not working for me.

I had become completely identified with the voice in my head and the incessant stream of involuntary and compulsive thinking and the emotions that accompanied it. Certain repetitive and persistent thoughts, emotions, and reactive patterns of behaviour were running my life.

Like most, I was strongly identified with a bundle of memories that I identified as 'Me and my story'. The habitual roles I played, mother, daughter, wife, business owner, all of these had been hot wired into my system by my family of origin, my environment and society since the day I was born, and I wasn't even aware it was these that were running the show.

That is when I discovered for myself the insane nature of Human Conditioning.

I discovered some powerful insights into what I now refer to as the **Human Control Codes**.

It wasn't long before I could see that it was these that were running my life, my behaviour and that were ultimately at the root of the unhappiness and hopelessness I had been feeling and experiencing for most of my life.

I started working with a business coach and within 3 weeks I started to experience some very real and profound changes happening in my life. This business coaching however was different to anything I had experienced before, the focus was on me not my business.

As a result, I slowed down, laughed more and generally felt I had a lot more space. I felt confident and in touch with myself, grounded and I had a sense of clarity that allowed me choice, so instead of reacting emotionally to the situations that arose, I now had the ability to take a breath, step back and evaluate from a place of space, and calm.

The best thing was it just kept getting better and better.

My life changed dramatically over the following months. I sold that cafe business (for a profit) and began concentrating full time on deactivating my Emotional Reactive Behaviour. I also started sharing the method with friends and their families.

What I love most about what I do now as a Behaviour Specialist and specifically the work I do with children with Anxiety or Behaviour Issues is that I get to facilitate REAL change within a relatively short period of time.

FEELINGS DRIVE BEHAVIOUR

The parents that call me at 8am in the morning in tears because they just can't get their child to co-operate enough to get them out the door to school or the parent whose child is not sleeping at night because they are having nightmares, or whose mind races so fast when they go to bed they are still wide-awake hours later.

Thousands of children are missing out on lots of lifes' little adventures because they have a fear or an anxiety. I get to teach them a tool that can change all of that, instantly.

Is your childs' constant bickering, tantrums and defiant behaviour embarrassing you, destroying your home environment and making you feel like a failure as a parent? Do you feel like you are living every parents' nightmare?

I am here to tell you that when you see through the behaviour to the underlying cause and use the tools and techniques I teach, you can deactivate the patterns of behaviour in your child and in yourself, quickly and easily.

The #1 Reason - Most other treatment options DON'T WORK is that they address the behaviour and the symptoms, not the Underlying cause!

Like covering a cut, with a Band-Aid, before cleaning the wound of infection.

It is not because you or your child is different or broken in some way, it's because everyone out there is trying to fix the behaviour. The **behaviour** is purely a **reaction** to a *feeling*, most other treatment options show you how to manage the behaviour or develop coping mechanisms and strategies to avoid triggering it in the first place.

They are all looking in the wrong place. Focused on the wrong things.
Feelings Drive Behaviour

It is important that you understand that when you remove the underlying cause the behaviour falls away and the need to strategize around it disappears.

REACTIVE, AGGRESSIVE BEHAVIOUR

As I experienced significant shifts in my own life I began offering this opportunity to parents with troubled children, my experience was that children didn't require the intellectual understanding that adults did, they trusted the process and experienced the shifts very quickly and easily.

I approached New Zealands' largest Intermediate school and spoke with their SENCO, Special Education Needs Coordinator. My exact words were; Give me your most Emotionally Challenged Child and I will give you a result!

There was one child they were struggling with, his behaviour was reactive, his attention span was short and he was being very disruptive in class, his school work was suffering and his relationships with the other students was being tested as they would tease him knowing they would get a reaction. These reactions had Liam visiting the headmaster at least once a day.

Liams' mum was feeling very hopeless with the situation, she had tried everything and Liams behaviour at home was testing her patience and resolve, she was willing and ready to try anything and she gave me permission to work with her son.

I connected quickly with Liam, he had the biggest most beautiful brown eyes, but they were filled with sadness and hurt. Mum and Dad had separated, and their relationship was far from amicable, Liam felt trapped and caught in the middle. He felt deep sadness and pressure, I helped him locate the energy inside his body and deactivate it. He was angry with his mum because he had to stay at her house rather than with Dad, I helped him Identify and locate where he held that energy and we Deactivated it. He suffered from dyslexia and found school work challenging he kept telling himself he was dumb and when others teased him calling him stupid he would lash out at the hurt. We Deactivated that too. Very quickly he became confident and very competent at Deactivating the incomplete emotional experiences and as he did his child like happiness returned, his energy became more playful and less serious and he started giggling. I went on to support Liam and his mum and sister for a few weeks but from that very first session Liam never returned to the headmasters' office for the remaining 2 years he attended the school. Because of the AMAZING results the school experienced I was able to return with various programmes and help more children understand that it was their Feelings that were driving their behaviour and I was able to give them techniques to process that energy more effectively.

My son Liam was struggling with school, he suffered learning difficulties (ADD & Dyslexia) with extreme emotional problems.

He was sensitive to negative feedback and perceived that he was teased and bullied more so than other children.

Despite all the intervention he received, he developed a true hatred for school and himself. Nothing seemed to work. He felt like no one could help him.

"It was just a waste of time"
He had given up and at times he became so overwhelmed by his emotions he was beyond reasoning and at times even threatening.

After the first half an hour introduction meeting with Becs he was a changed boy. He walked out of her office with a bounce in his step, shoulders pulled back, head held high and a playful smile on his face. I think he even did a twirl. For the first time in a long time my son was Free.

I had booked Liam and his sister, Tayla into Rebeccas' school holiday programme for emotional health, he couldn't wait to get back to his session with Becs.

Both children were counting down the days.

Even after the workshop Liam was keen to work with Becs again. He was looking for a reason why he would need to see her again.

It was like all of his anxieties and fears that caused his extreme emotional reaction had gone. He was no longer living in fear. Fear of being bullied or teased.

He no longer has that extreme reaction when something happens to him in the class and the playground.

He deals with his issues calmly and rationally.

Liam has a new-found strength within himself allowing him the courage to try new things, explore possibilities and to take a risk.
He is not afraid to be himself, despite what others may say, it is truly like my son is free.

"It was really good and will help you Heaps"~Liam

Sharon Foley

Sick With Worry

One of my first private clients was a young boy, 13 years old, who had been experiencing some quite serious health issues and food allergies. He was becoming thin and withdrawn, and socially disinterested. He was missing a lot of school and his grades were falling. His parents had tried everything. They had been to see numerous different doctors and specialists for his health and he had been seeing a school counsellor for his anxieties. Things were not getting any better, in fact they were getting worse. They were at a complete loss as to what to do next and where to turn, there just seemed to be no explanation for his ill health and behaviour and they were worried sick!

As we introduced ourselves, they told me of their transient lifestyle over the last 2 years following the Christchurch Earthquake, here in New Zealand. I turned to the boy and asked excitedly 'What was it like to experience the quake?'

The look of panic in his eyes was a clear indication to me as to where there was an incomplete emotional experience and perhaps the source of the current ill health.

This child was caught in a pattern of fear. No further words were spoken all that I need to do was lead this young boy towards the sensatns he was feeling in his body. As the session ended he started to giggle, the colour had returned to his face and his posture was relaxed and comfortable. He opened his eyes and looked straight at me;

"You know the quake hit at 4am? Well Dad doesn't wear anything to bed, so when he came to get me I saw things jiggling and shaking that no one should ever have to see!"

His mum sent me a text me out of the blue about 4 months later;

"Just been to parent/teacher interviews for G. G as you know missed most of last year due to ill health. He is now year 9. We didn't know if he would be ok this year due to missing so much of year 8! We were in tears of joy. He is thriving, topping all his classes. We are stunned at the % All above 80%. This is a boy who struggled in primary. Thank you so much for your help. He's even in the school rock band! So cool Happy Boy ☺"

Thanks Julie

PRIMAL RESPONSES TO DANGER

We all carry around with us a huge reservoir of accumulated negative feelings, attitudes and beliefs as a result of our experiences and our primal response to danger and fear, this is sometimes refered to as our *Emotional Baggage*.

The accumulated pressure makes us miserable and sometimes makes us want to lash out at the world around us or run away and hide from it. Most people spend their time trying to avoid and run away from this inner turmoil of fear and anger and from the threat of the misery they feel inside.

We have 3 Primal responses to Danger (Fear):

1. Fight
2. Flight
3. Freeze

And these play out in the 5 major ways that we process our feelings. Feelings are just our emotional response to Danger and Fear.

1. Suppression
2. Repression
3. Expression
4. Distraction
5. Escape

Suppression

Suppression happens consciously. We don't want to be bothered by feelings, we are not quite sure what to do with them, so we hide them away. When we are little we can become very afraid of our feelings because they hold such a massive amount of negativity. We fear we will become overwhelmed by the emotion if we face it. We are so scared that we just won't be able to handle the emotion, so we put a lid on it, stuff it down or suffer through it trying to function the best way that we can.

It is a conscious choice not to indulge a particular thought, feeling, or action. 'Not to indulge' means that we are aware of a thought or feeling, but we decide not to dwell on it (internally, by continuing to think about it) nor to express it (externally, by acting it out).

Suppression is a useful psychological mechanism which permits us to concentrate on our activities without being distracted by every impulse which arises and without having the need to act on those impulses. We acknowledge the impulses and we accept their presence and the fact that they might emerge again, to be reconciled or suppressed again. Continued suppression of this emotional energy leads to general anxiety and we appear to others as stressed and anxious. In some cases, children (and adults) develop strategies to cope with the internal pressure and these can quickly become OCD, repeated behaviour patterns used to prevent the feelings from surfacing and potentially overwhelming us.

Repression

When we repress a feeling, it is because there is so much guilt and fear at having the feeling that it is not even consciously felt at all. Repression is similar to suppression in that a thought or feeling or emotion is not expressed, but in repression, we deny that the element even exists. The repressed element might come into our conscious awareness and then be denied, or it might be prohibited from our awareness. It is blocked because it has been judged to be so potentially disruptive and damaging to our psychological stability or our self-image that we could not possibly handle the way it would make us feel if we were to face it.

Repression can be a useful defence mechanism. Although repression is generally viewed as detrimental, it is rightly called a "defence mechanism" because it defends us against psychological material which we believe might indeed be dangerous if we don't have the strength or ability to face the overwhelm.

Whether repressed or suppressed, the elements remain intact and energized; they continue to influence us while they push for Expression. Although suppression can cause tension and conflict, repression can cause even more damage particularly because our 'unawareness' of it means that we have less ability to recognize the ways in which it is affecting us and harming us. The strain of these internalised experiences create so much internal pressure they start to manifest in daily life as severe anxiety, phobias, PTSD, panic disorder and physical illnesses.

Our perceptions become distorted. While the repressed material is in the shadow, it projects onto people and situations; for example, fear which has been repressed when projected will colour our perceptions of the world as a frightening place. Repressed anger may become deep resentment and bitterness causing us to push people away only intensifying the feeling of isolation. Because we are not perceiving accurately, we acquire incorrect information from our surroundings, and thus we respond inappropriately; we react fearfully to situations which are not truly dangerous.

Repression distorts not only our observations in this moment, but also it colours our memories of the past and our expectations for the future. Repression consumes energy. The effort to keep material in the unconscious mind is like the effort to keep a buoyant object underwater; we are using energy to hold back the energy of the repressed elements. When repressed material is released, we might experience a feeling of lightness and freedom and power, because the energy from the incomplete experience and from our effort to repress it is now available for a constructive use.

I offer my clients a step by step proven process that identifies and deactivates suppressed and repressed emotional energy. Getting directly to the source and eliminating the root cause of the behaviour. I don't treat or teach you or your child how to manage the behaviour, whatever form it takes. I teach you and your child how to identify Patterns of Behaviour conscious or subconscious Supressed or Repressed and then how to deactivate them systematically. Giving both more internal space and happiness by releasing tension and stress that is held in the body and this provides an increased feeling of personal power.

Expression

Expression is what has been labelled as Disruptive Behaviour Disorders and include Oppositional Defiant Disorder (ODD), Conduct Disorder (CD) and Attention Deficit Hyperactivity Disorder (ADHD). Typical behaviours associated with these disorders include becoming easily angered or annoyed or irritated, frequent temper tantrums, arguing frequently with adults particularly the most familiar adults in their lives, such as parents. Refusal to obey rules, the child seems to deliberately try to annoy or aggravate others, low self-esteem, low frustration threshold and continually seeks to blame others for any misfortunes or misdeeds.

A sufferer of ADHD is said to have inattention – difficulty concentrating, forgetting instructions, moving from one task to another without completing anything. Being Impulsive, talking over the top of others, having a 'short fuse' and being accident prone. Overactivity – constant restlessness and fidgeting.

AN EXAMPLE OF EXTREME BEHAVIOUR

I want to share a relevant quick story about one of my private clients whose primary way of handling his feelings was through Expression and displayed many of the tendencies listed. This method of handling emotions, results in the feelings being expressed verbally or in aggressive actions, allowing just enough of the pressure out while the rest stays suppressed. Like letting air out of an over inflated balloon to stop it from popping. His behaviour allowed enough of the pressure of the Incomplete Emotion to be let out allowing the remainder to be suppressed.

He was 12 years old and had been in the 'System' since he was 6 years old and he displayed extreme behaviours – diagnosed and medicated for ADHD and ODD, but still displaying disrespectful often violent behaviour. Verbally abusive towards his mum and stepdad, his younger brother was often in the line of fire. At school disrespect of teachers and peers and fighting or bullying had him visiting the headmaster's office regularly and although very talented on the sports field he was not allowed to take part in team events because of his reactive behaviour.

The school had just had enough of the child's behaviour and The Ministry of Education Wraparound Services was brought in to deal with the situation.

They reached out to me to work with the child and his mother, who by now was totally at the end of her tether and was threatening to physically discipline him if something didn't change soon.

After 1 session with the child and the mother, there was a noticeable change in them both and within the first week, the Educational psychologist in charge of the case documented a 70% decrease in behaviour incidents at home and 100% decrease at school. Everyone around them was noticing and commenting on the observable difference in behaviour and attitude, both were happier and less stressed, mum reported to actually quite liking her child again.

Now 6 months down the line with further 1:1 coaching sessions they are closer and happier than ever before, both taking responsibility for their own emotional state and using the tools as and when necessary to deactivate any further conditioned responses that arise. The school note that this child is now a valued member of the class and school community and is cooperative and collaborative with his peers, enjoying a healthy school and home life and representing his school in soccer and basketball. Mum has been promoted at work and is trying for another child. Little brother is enjoying having a loving and supportive older brother. The relationship with his stepdad is much better.

The key was helping them discover that the child's behaviour was just his way of expressing and letting out internal emotional pressure. Once he was shown how to identify and deactivate the source, the behaviour was no longer needed, because the build-up of pressure had gone from inside him, almost immediately the behaviour outbursts at home and school decreased.

The behaviour had been learnt. It was not until I started working with both the child and his mother that I could see the similarity in their behaviour, although mums' behaviour was in some respect "more adult", the disrespectful and aggressive nature was obvious to and felt by everyone but her. Her behaviour too had been learned and the mechanisms and ways of coping with the emotional overwhelm she had developed as part of her own childhood conditioning.

So if there are days when you just want to strangle your child, not go home because you are too exhausted to deal with the drama, feel hopeless because nothing seems to work and think there isn't anything you can do to get them to change.

There is HOPE, answers and a practical solution to help you have the well-behaved child you've been longing for.

Prior to meeting Rebecca, I was at my wits end, I had a child that was in turmoil, disrespectful, emotional, diagnosed ADHD and ODD with sensory overload. We are a blended family and I had completed every parenting programme you could think off. We had in home support, psychologists, ICHAMS (yes, he was medicated) in place.

I wanted him fixed, to me he was broken. We also had Intensive Wraparound Service support through Ministry of Education, we had teacher aides 24/7 at school just to keep him there, he was on his last legs at school and was close to being expelled.

I cringed prior to morning wake ups and dreaded school collection. Every day it was an explosive mess that would last hours and result in damaging property or lashing out at us.
I snapped one day and as a mother I was like OMG and I hit him! I felt terrible how could I as a mother let myself go, I felt that I had no hope left, I was open to anything to help my family.

At that time the blame was always on my son I didn't take responsibility as "it was all his fault what did I do to deserve this".

I was approached by the SENCO (Special Education Needs Coordinator) at school who asked me if I would I be willing to work with Rebecca as an alternative?

I said that I would do anything. I was at a point in my life where I had been battling this behaviour for 7 years and I couldn't or didn't want to do it any more, I was even considering giving my child away. I was angry within myself, my marriage was affected it was affecting our whole lives and our younger child. I started to hate my own child it was true I loved him but hated him at the same time, all I ever wanted was to love my son again.

So the journey with Rebecca began, when I first met Rebecca I listened to her but thought to myself WTF is this mumbo jumbo crap about. I had just completed my Degree and with the training I completed for my job I found myself trying to analyse what she was talking about, find evidence for the madness, but there wasn't any.

Rebecca worked with me and my son for about 3 months intensively. We went through and Deactivated our Human Control Codes. It wasn't until I was almost 3/4 of the way through that I realized that I played a huge role in my sons emotional turmoil as we would feed off each other. I used to get emotional and cry or lash out. I was my sons biggest advocate and I would fight for him but in a negative way, aggressive and reactive and emotionally driven behaviour, I don't any more, I still feel emotional, but I can manage my emotions so much better.

I identified a lot of my inner emotions were driven from my own personal journey. I was raised right but spent a lot of years in hospital, due to a birth defect in one of my legs. I was protected but this was a negative experience for me as I felt I wasn't perfect, even though I was very much loved, looking back now I think my mum must have been feeling like I was feeling being a mother. I did not love my self and because of this I engaged in unhealthy relationships with men.

I had done all the courses for this but had never dealt with the underlying emotion that was entrenched in me nor had I dealt with the negative experiences I had had with family violence. Once I felt things fully I was able to complete the emotional overwhelm I was experiencing and I was no long being driven by the underlying emotional energy.

I have had so many good things happen to me since I started seeing Rebecca, my job is better, my relationship with my children is better, my family and clients see me in a different light now. I have had so many comments from other agencies and professionals I work with who say I am easier to approach and work with now, I used to put up a "don't mess with me or its over persona" even though that is not who I am, it was how I came across.

I feel Rebecca has saved my life and with that I thank you, don't get me wrong my life is far from perfect but it is a hell of a way forward from where I was at, my son still displays behaviours but nowhere near as bad and I am in a way better place to manage that, we both are. If you ever get the opportunity to work with Rebecca give it 100% don't fight the emotions it may just save your life.

Jena Young
Registered Social Worker
Coordinator for Whare4Whanau Emergency Housing Provider

DISTRACTION OR ESCAPE

Distraction or Escape is the 4th major way we have learnt to handle our emotions. This is the **flight** response. When we were very young our nervous system was fragile and still developing and prone to overwhelm. We had to learn pretty quickly how to deal with the overwhelming feelings that we had inside that felt uncomfortable and that we didn't want to have to face.

We are programmed from the beginning.

One of the main ways we deal with babies that are emotionally overwhelmed is through Distraction. We distract them away from the overwhelmed with a sound or a touch or a visual distraction and then, because it is more comfortable we end up defaulting into these patterns of distraction subconsciously.

We learn to stay unconscious and distracted rather than face this possible overwhelm. Our most common methods of distraction are to turn to social media and TV, drugs and alcohol. The entire entertainment industry is built around our need to escape from feeling unwanted feelings.

Most of us dread a moment of aloneness so we fill our lives with a constant stream of frantic activities, endless socialising, talking, texting, reading, music playing, working, traveling, sightseeing, shopping, over-eating, gambling, movie-going, pill taking, drug using and drinking. It is theses addictive activities that provide a distraction from feeling. We also distract ourselves with drama and internal storytelling. We tell ourselves stories ALL the time and if we attach too strongly with stories of things we've done or that have happened to us in the past as negative or unwanted. There is a tendency to develop depression as the focus is on stuff that makes us feel sad or guilty or ashamed.

These feelings can become so intense and compounded the release comes in physical self-harming and in the most extreme cases suicide. These stories can provide a mechanism of withdrawal and escape for the individual who is so afraid of the inner turmoil and emotional energy they have inside their bodies.

The link between behaviour and emotions is not a new one and there are many trains of thought around how to deal with it. I approach things a little differently.

In the work that I have done with my private clients and particularly with the children, Anxiety is the main player.

Anxiety occurs as the result of being stuck at the outer edges of fear - afraid, in a sense, of the deeper, overwhelming energy of fear.

Anxiety is a MASSIVE problem.

It is the most common mental illness in the US with 1 in 7 adults struggling with anxiety on an ongoing basis and in the most part it is going untreated. Prescription medications and Psychotherapy have been the go to in the past and the problem just seems to be getting worse. Children as young as 6 years old are experiencing the onset of Anxiety and ADHD. Increasing numbers of youth are becoming involved in violent behaviour with alcohol and drugs being a component in this escalation. Suicide here in New Zealand is on the increase.

This is an epidemic and it is accelerating.

The physical symptoms of Anxiety are:

- Hot and cold flushes
- Shaking
- Racing heart
- Tight feeling in the chest or chest pain in extreme cases
- Struggle to find the next breath
- Worries snowballing, getting bigger and bigger so our mind races or feels jumbled
- Feel our head might explode with all the thoughts
- An intense pressure or feeling we need to check things are done correctly or are clean.

All of these symptoms have a **sensation** associated with them, a physical reaction to a stimulus, and that stimuli in the case of Anxiety is a thought.

Anxiety is our body's response to a thought.

If the thoughts are negative and fear based and the threat is not a REAL threat, it is only perceived or a made-up outcome.

Most of these beliefs and patterns were generated in our childhood, and we grow up believing we are not *good enough, pretty enough, fast enough, clever enough.*
The Fear causes internal pressure and we develop coping strategies and methods to manage, control or escape from the internal pressure.

The internal pressure is caused by incomplete emotional experiences from our early-childhood that have been coded into our *Main Frame* at a *Feeling Level* and produced a pattern of behaviour.

Most other methods and solutions available teach you further coping mechanisms, ways to manage, control or escape from the internal pressure.

I teach you HOW To Deactivate the source code and then the pattern of behaviour simply falls away. It is a very simple and a very effective way to deal with all behaviours.

You may believe that you just have to learn to live with your anxiety or watch your child suffer and there is nothing that can be done, it's just the way you are!

Or perhaps you believe it just runs in the family, it is genetic or maybe you believe that medication is the only option!

I am here to tell you that the only reason you experience anxiety is because you haven't learned to effectively resolve intense emotions or traumas.

It is as simple as learning to do the exact opposite of what you have been taught and conditioned to do!

Unless that trauma is dealt with on the level it was put in, it will continue to run the show from the subconscious.

We have daily emotional trauma as we are growing up and because we have no other means to deal with it we employ strategies to help us cope until one day we are put under so much strain that our coping mechanisms stop working for us or the strain becomes too much to bare and the cracks begin to appear.

When you understand the root cause of that anxiety and behaviour, you will be able to deactivate it quickly and easily leaving you and your child, happy and relaxed, less stressed and not fearful of what may or may not happen.

This gives you a sense of freedom and space.

Just imagine not feeling under constant pressure!

Let's take a look at Anxiety a little closer.

There are 5 distinct forms of anxiety and these are categorised by the intensity of the feelings and sensations:

General Anxiety Disorder

This is when people worry about a number of things. The stats show that this occurs mostly in young adults and women more than men. The anxiety is about a wide range of situations and issues, not just one specific event. We don't seem to have any control over the thoughts and they find their way into all parts of daily life affecting our appetite, our sleep and even our recreational time.

Phobias

Phobias are extreme and irrational fear about a particular thing. They can be so frightening that the person goes to great lengths to avoid that particular thing, even if it is harmless. Social phobia is a fear of being judged or embarrassed in public, agoraphobia is not just a fear of open spaces but can also be related to being away from a safe place or a person who makes you feel safe.

Claustrophobia is the fear of confined spaces or being trapped without the possibility of being able to get out. Often a fear of flying is less about the fear of the plane crashing but a fear of being confined to small space that you are unable to get out of.

Phobias and the associated sensations can be so intense and disabling it can leave people unable to leave their home.

Obsessive Compulsive Disorder (OCD)

This is when a person has intrusive, persistent unwanted repetitive thoughts, that trigger feelings and sensations in an attempt to counteract these thoughts, a repetitive action or ritual is devised by the person to help alleviate the internal pressure they feel. For example, someone who is afraid of germs, relieves the internal pressure from the repeated thought pattern by washing their hands, again and again or refuses to touch door handles with their bare hands. It can be very distressing (although before it became an entrenched pattern of behaviour it was developed to make us feel safe) and can get in the way of school, work and normal life at home.

Post-traumatic Stress Disorder (PTSD)

This is a reaction to a highly stressful event outside the range of everyday experience when a person feels very unsafe or threatened (a response to Danger / Fear).

PTSD is the body's response to these traumatic experiences, war, and natural disasters, violent attacks (verbal, physical or sexual). The symptoms are intense reactions to the stimuli and include heightened anxiety, flashbacks, nightmares, startle response and people usually increasingly avoid situations that might trigger these responses causing them to feel alone, isolated and their quality of life becomes severely compromised.

Panic Disorder

Panic attacks are very frightening and uncomfortable as the sensations associated with anxiety become increasingly intense and overwhelming, pounding heart, feeling faint, sweating, shaking limbs, nausea, chest pains breathing discomfort and an exaggerated feeling of being out of control. The symptoms can rise and peak rapidly and often people feel like they are dying (although as frightening as these symptoms feel they are not in fact life threatening.

CONFLICTING BEHAVIOUR

By understanding the inner conflicts your child is struggling with and how they were activated early in their childhood, you will begin to understand the source of the current behaviour and how these patterns of behaviour and belief systems developed in early childhood are running the show for most of us. I can show you how to identify them and deactivate them so that your child can move through the limiting belief patterns and start creating the life of their dreams.

Just imagine having fun and laughing again with your child and your family, interacting in a relaxed open way, not afraid that something you say will spark them into running off to their room in tears or a huff to be alone, not wanting to tell you what has really upset them or what's on their minds.

Imagine sleeping soundly through the night because you are not tossing and turning worried because your child seems isolated and alone, alienating themselves from their friends their family and especially from you and spending more and more time lost in social media.

If you just don't know what to do to help your child, and you want them to open up and talk, there is something vital you need to know.

The issue was INPUT on a feeling level and therefore it has to be addressed on the same level, the feeling level.

You can't change a feeling by understanding it with a thought.

An Inner Conflict is when our natural intention or intuition, (which is our ability to understand something instinctively without the need for conscious reasoning) is blocked by a conditioned or learnt response.

In order to understand this, we need to understand how our preverbal conditioning affects us.

Every human experience is composed of three fundamental components:

1. Experiencer (US)
2. Object of Experience
3. Process of Experiencing

Together these three make up all our Experiences.

When we are very young we have all sorts of experiences that conflict with our natural desires and intentions. A late feed, cold legs, needing comforting and in some cases, much more traumatic experiences. Whatever it was, these experiences are often too much for our delicate systems to process. So, in an attempt to 'handle it' we may start to identify too strongly with the thing we are experiencing, the cold, the hunger, the need for a cuddle and, we CODE into our system that there is a crucial part of ourselves that is missing or broken and we need someone or something to make it better, or fix it for us.

Many people, if not all of us, spend our life time searching for the something or someone to make the FEELING go away.

As we became independent and able to meet our own needs that feeling still persists and we spend our lives looking for something that was never missing in the first place!

Our EGOs develop when we identify too strongly with our notions of who we think we are, we have the tendency to identify with our collection of life stories, accomplishments, disappointments, traumas, pleasures and all other life experiences. It's the behaviour everyone around us is displaying so it is pretty difficult not to be influenced by this modelling.

However, it leads us to **Input code** on a feeling level that we are an isolated individual, we find ourselves feeling separate from and constantly fighting with the world around us, and we develop behaviours to defend our sense of SELF (EGO).

Now if we find ourselves identifying too strongly with the actual process of experiencing itself, then we will often find ourselves overwhelmed by emotions, crying all the time or just feeling angry, stressed and frustrated. We tend to use; antidepressants, alcohol, drugs, work and exercise as ways to keep ourselves away from the Overwhelm.

The confusion and frustration increase when we have a combination going on; when we identify with our EGO but also strongly identify with the feeling that part of ourselves is missing.

Look at me look at me! Don't look at me... Over here. I said don't look at me!

This is an **Internal Conflict** and leads us to feel we are living a life of constant struggle as our EGO demands to be recognised while we desperately try to become absent in the face of strong overwhelming emotions!

All of this 'behaviour' is taught to us through our conditioning, so it is our conditioning that is running the show, and most of the time you are not aware that's what is going on!

This is the insidious nature of Conditioning!

I can show you how to liberate your child from the limitations of their conditioning.

SELF-HARMING, SUICIDAL TEEN

A distraught mum, brought her 14-year-old daughter to me because she was really concerned about her daughter's behaviour. Her behaviour was becoming quite dark, she was shutting herself off from the family and spending a lot of time in her room on social media. She wasn't sleeping well, often pacing round the house and the streets in the early hours of the morning because she was unable to sleep and then being tired and lethargic through the day refusing to go to school. The velocity of her manic mood swings was resulting in her hurting or harming herself. On this one particular occasion after spending time with my private client, I uncovered she had broken her own arm to get out of having to visit her Dad and stepmum.

She had such huge inner conflict and was suppressing so much emotional energy around what she was experiencing. She was so desperate not to upset her Dad but was becoming increasingly concerned by how much her Dad and stepmum drank each night, and how verbally abusive her stepmum became towards her after drinking. She felt deeply hurt and let down by her Dad, who in her eyes would not stand up for or defend her, and was often coerced into joining in the Adult Bad Behaviour!

This had triggered self-worth and self-esteem issues for my client.

Using my method of locating the underlying feeling in the body, I asked her to simply notice how it made her feel, heavy in her heart, a lump in her throat and the stinging of tears behind her eyes, all these sensations were present. She became aware that she would fight back the tears, swallow through the lump in her throat and remove herself to her room where she could distract herself from the ache in her heart. She also became aware that she would avoid these feelings by isolating herself or by coming up with reason to not go to Dads place, even going to the extent of making herself ill or harming herself. When the sensations were acknowledged and the energy deactivated, the patterns of avoidance were disengaged.

My client was then able to communicate with some family friends who arranged an intervention with her Dad and stepmum where they addressed the situation. The drinking stopped and with it the verbal abuse. My private client started opening up to her Mum and Dad again, talking and sharing with clear, open communication.

My daughter was 14 when she met Rebecca for the first time, I've known Rebecca for a few years prior to that. And my daughter was in deep depression, she was suicidal, We just didn't know what to do with her.

I called Rebecca and thankfully she fitted us in urgently that day, made space for her, and with a 1-hour session, coming out from that session, my daughter had a different view on life. She said I feel so much better. Now that didn't, obviously one session didn't fix everything when somebody is in that state of mind. It's a hard place to get out of especially if you've got other external factors happening in your environment that you're not in control of when young.

She saw Rebecca quite intensively weekly and then monthly. This kid is just a different kid now; she is a young woman who knows what she wants. She left school, she has done an art and design certificate and she's on her way to doing a studying an Art degree next year.
She has confidence, she can stand up for herself, she can speak the truth. There are so many things that she couldn't do, she couldn't be fully expressed before. Whatever Rebecca did or said or brought out in her has been the biggest gift as a mum that I could ever know, and I can't thank you enough Rebecca, because you saved my daughter's life.

If you have a child or even if you're a young adult and you need some help and you think that all is lost, then go and see Rebecca, because I can't recommend her enough.

Pam Roska - Midwife

If your childs behaviour is concerning you and you sense there is something driving it, but just don't know what to do or what to say to get them to open up to you. Or, if you just want to reconnect with your child again and have them talk to you, even through their teenage years, read on.

We all experience internal conflict when we know what we want but there appears to be an invisible force preventing us from achieving our goals. This is because we have deep seated insidious layers of Conditioning and Coding in place that keep us caught in Internal Conflict between our Natural Intentions and our Conditioned Response.

This deep layer of insidious conditioning keeps us stuck in Struggle, Isolation and Frustration. It was INPUT before we had words to explain it or even understand it. What we call the **Human Control Codes** have imposed many limitations in your life and in that of your child.

EARLY CHILDHOOD LESSONS?

How the coding was put in place:

Modelling

We model our behaviour or attitudes on those of a parent or primary caregiver. We learn **ways of being** directly from them by osmosis, which is the gradual and unconscious soaking up of ideas and knowledge we experience around us.

Teaching

Our parents or primary caregivers teach us a certain way of being is the RIGHT or WRONG way to be.

Discipline

Our parents or primary caregivers discipline us when we acted in a certain way, so we have made a conscious effort to act in the opposite way to avoid the punishment. Later this way of being becomes unconscious.

Internalization of a critic

Our parent or primary caregiver were critical of you so a part of you (your EGO) took on that same attitude towards yourself.

Fortune Telling

This occurs when they predict that things will turn out badly using language like:

- I know I will fail the exam.
- I just know I will miss the goal.

However, you know we cannot predict the future because we don't have a magic ball.

Overgeneralizing

This is when they use words like 'always' or 'never' to describe situations or events. This is a problematic way of thinking because it does not take all situations or events into account. For example, sometimes we may make mistakes, but we don't 'always' make mistakes.

Mind-reading

This happens when they believe that they know what others are thinking and they assume that they are thinking the worst of them.

- They think I am stupid
- She doesn't like me

However, we can't mind-read, so we can't know what others are thinking

Labelling

Sometimes they talk to themselves in a mean way and use a single negative word to describe themselves;

- I am stupid
- I am a failure

This kind of thinking is unfair, and we are too complex to be summed up in a single word.

Filtering

This happens when they take note of all the bad things that happen but ignore any of the good things.

And

Overestimating

This happens when they imagine the worst possible thing is about to happen and they will be unable to cope with it.

- I'll embarrass myself and everyone will laugh
- I'll freak out and no one will help

All of these cause our children to become caught up in mental traps and as a parent it is helpful to be aware of them.

We all fall into these traps when we are children and many of us are still caught inside of them, listen to your own mental chatter and the language you use, is there a pattern you see that your child is displaying too?

THE HUMAN CONTROL CODES

Understanding the Patterns of Behaviour that run your Life

It didn't take me long to recognise that the source of my suffering and human suffering for that matter, was to be found in society today as Emotional Incompetence. The vast majority, if not all of our social, economic and financial problems have a direct and deep-seated root in our inability to deal with and process our emotions.

It was my lack of emotional competence that was the root cause of the problems in my life and as you read on I am sure you too will recognise as the problems that most of us experience in our lives. It is the underlying cause of unemployment, crime, addictions, many wellness/health care problems, anxiety, depression, low productivity, parenting issues and relationship problems. In fact there is hardly an area of life that is unaffected by, simply, our inability to handle our emotions effectively.

Using a set of twelve insights into human conditioning as a map and using some very simple techniques that I was taught to complete incomplete emotions, I was able to start the process of releasing myself from the insidious conditioned patterns of behaviour that subconsciously had been running my life and I suspect are presently running yours and your childs.

This set of insights provides the answer to the question – What's really going on? They make conscious the unconscious patterns of conditioning that are mostly pre-verbal (set down in the very early stages of life) and provide a map for getting to the real underlying basis of any problem.

Let us see if you can identify with the influence of any of these Control Codes.

SO SCARED SHE COULDN'T SPEAK

I received a call one day from a very distraught mum.

"My daughter just can't stop crying and I don't know what to do, I can't help her, please will you help?"

Maddy was 9 when she came to see me. She was very quiet and shy, withdrawn and scared looking. She sat in my big leather recliner biting her lip and wringing her hands. When I asked her what was wrong she just looked up at me with tear filled eyes and simply shook her head.

Using your hands Maddy can you show me how big it feels? She stretched her arms as far as she could and then shaking her head she started sobbing again. By the end of the first session she still could not tell me what was upsetting her but the size of the overwhelm she showed me had reduce by more than half. She used the technique I had taught her over the next couple of days and her mum brought her back. Her demeanour had lightened, and I got a gentle smile as she sat back into the leather recliner, using her hands again she indicated that the energy remaining was less than quarter of the original size.

I introduced her to another technique and after about 20mins her eyes flicked open and she said;

"What if something happens to mum when she is away and Dad dies, who is going to look after me?"

Her FEAR had been huge. Dad had been diagnosed with a brain tumour and although he was receiving treatment the prognosis wasn't good. Mum had to go on an overseas trip and poor Maddy was so overwhelmed by the feelings that she had been unable to vocalise what was going on for her.

This coping mechanism is the **Human Control Code** known as *Resisting Feeling Things Fully* and it is the Fear of Emotional Overwhelm. When we are very little we all get emotionally overwhelmed. You know the feeling. It is often so raw, uncomfortable and traumatic that we tend to make a 'feeling-level-decision' to put a lid on it, push it down and away to avoid having to feel the awful experience of overwhelm.

We are trying to avoid having to feel intense emotions fully, in fact we suppress them, so we feel as little as possible, if at all. Why? Because at the time we were scared, and it was painful, it was the best response we had at the time and it seems to be universal. In other words, everyone seems to make this pre-verbal decision, it is just part of being human.

Unfortunately, what we do after making this feeling level decision is that we begin to build our life around strategies of avoidance in order to minimize the awful experience of feeling the intensity of the emotions and becoming emotionally overwhelmed.

Now that Maddy had the tools and the techniques to Identify and Deactivate the emotional energy that was building up, she was now able to express her concerns, she was able to communicate her uncertainty and voice the questions she had. The practicalities of the situation were explained.

Maddy and I had another couple of sessions where we talked and identified other areas of her life that were causing her internal pressure. By the end of our coaching time together Maddy was back to being happy and chatty, she was in fact now looking forward to the time with her grandparents while mum was away, and she had become a class mentor after displaying compassion and open communication skills with some class mates who were bullying and being mean to others. Maddys' mum had a very enjoyable worry-free trip. Maddys' dad did pass away soon after, but she continued to process the emotional energy that was arising, and she remains a happy healthy thriving 12-year-old.

When we ***Resist Feeling Things Fully*** we have an inclination not to complete intense emotional experiences. Instead we just stuff them down and put a lid on them. We start packing our Emotional Baggage for the trip of our lifetime.

We hold that energy inside our bodies and if we stop for just one moment, we have this sense that it will all come crashing in! So, we keep busy, distracted, out of the moment, we keep ourselves **Distracted.** For it is in the present moment that the patterns of energy begin to press into our awareness demanding to be felt and completed. We are so afraid of the emotional overwhelm we start adopting all sorts of behaviours to avoid the emotional pain.

DESPERATE WITH NOWHERE TO TURN

Ollie was one of the first kids I worked with while I was learning how to take other people through the process I had discovered. Ollie and his mum had spent nearly two years going through the 'System' with Ollies OCD (Obsessive Compulsive Disorder). They had seen numerous councillors and phycologists and no one could help. They could label it, tell you what it was, where and when it started and perhaps even why it had started, but they couldn't tell them how to stop it. Medication had become the final option.

When Ollie visited me for the first time he sat up straight, feeling all important in my big leather recliner. My first thought was; 'boy this kids' knees are REALLY dirty!" From the shin to his thigh on both legs he was covered in grass stains and mud. He obviously went all in when playing sport!'

Ollie counted on his fingers, rapidly, all the time, while he was playing rugby, doing his homework, watching TV, even in class when doing his maths. At the same time he would be counting in his head the number of letters in the last word he had heard (but … only if he could spell it) and then he would count each letter out on his fingers. It was actually mind blowing what he was doing and still managing to function at a high level. The teachers and psychologists were astounded!

Within one session the finger counting had stopped!
ONE SESSION!

I took him through a very quick painless process that identified the underlying cause and then I taught him how to deactivate it. And just like his sport, because of his 'all in' nature, he trusted the process fully and he didn't hold back. After our first session the fingers remained uncounted for nearly 7hrs!

I collected him from school the following day at lunch time (his mum was working and there wasn't a way for her to bring him to me) Ollie and I worked through a few more energies, each time he released one, his whole energy would shift, he would become lighter and more open. Again, the finger counting stopped and this time it wouldn't return.

I uncovered that at the root cause of Ollies OCD was an emotional pain he was trying to avoid feeling, the pain of his parents separating had been too much for him to process and he had created this pattern of behaviour to avoid having to feel the emotions he could sense were lurking inside.

Rebecca was a saving grace for my son aged eight, who developed an OCD condition due to anxiety caused by life happening out of his control. This condition was taken to the public health system coming to no avail. I was given Rebecca's number and Ollie visited her twice, before we could see my son back again, with confidence and happiness. My son was such a confident kid with awesome leadership skills, fearless and out going. The anxiety made all of these attributes go away, and Rebecca gave my son the tools to get them back again.

My son got to the point of wanting to change schools, and even saying things like, "this habit is ruining my life!", which of course would break any mothers heart. He was being bullied.

Rebecca taught my son tools for life to deal with incomplete emotions, fears and anxieties.

Thankyou Rebecca, my son is back and happy as ever with his confidence blooming.

As for the OCD habbit that was causing his lack of confidence, it has GONE!

From a very grateful Mum

Thankyou Rebecca for getting rid of my fears and helping me to not do my habit.

You should go see Rebecca to make your problems go away.

Thank you Rebecca
From a very grateful little boy

The **Fear of Emotional Overwhelm** leads to us *Avoiding the Present* or *Getting Distracted.*

It is indeed one of the most common emotional traumas I help children to process.

I also hear it said a lot, *"he makes me feel sad, she makes me feel angry"*.

This is another behaviour we learn from a very young age. Just by observing and modelling the behaviours of those around us, we become very judgemental of not only others but also judgemental of ourselves. This is the voice of the Internal Critic.

Let's get something straight, **No-one,** has the power to make us feel anything. It is **always** a choice to feel a certain way.

Take a moment just to let that sink in.

Where do the feelings occur?

They originate inside of us. Others may trigger those feelings for us, but no one can make us feel a certain way. We have learned through experience and observation that it is so much easier and less painful to judge the feeling as something bad or wrong in someone else than acknowledge that this uncomfortable energy actually sits inside of us.

We don't want to feel this deep discomfort so we develop a tendency to express our distaste, our judgmental feelings, towards the other person or situation rather than feeling the feeling inside ourselves. We are actually taught to do this, by our family, society, media, social media and the world around us, it has us comparing ourselves to others and judging.

MOTHER SON RELATIONSHIP

A dear friend of mine, was very keen to attend a live business event in the United States but was terrified of flying. We Deactivated that fear for Dave in less than 30mins. He flew out of Auckland airport in hurricane force winds with a smile on his face and when he arrived at the event in New York he was buzzing, telling anyone who would listen about the process that blitzed his fear so quickly.

MattyD was at that event and became my first international private client, after experiencing his own fear of flying being deactivated in less than 30mins, he was hooked. Based in Maryland, USA, we would meet weekly on skype and I would coach Matt through any issues that had arisen for him throughout the week, we coached like that for almost 2 years and Matt now has his own coaching practise and YouTube channel.

When we started deactivating energy after energy after energy, it wasn't long before a pattern of behaviour we know as **Being Judgemental** became quite clear especially in his relationship with his mother. He'd say things like;

"She always makes me feel like I am a looser, and she always asks me when I am going to stop messing up and get a real job? No, I haven't told her I have a girlfriend are you insane? Man she makes me angry, I can't even to talk to her right now!"

Once we had isolated these patterns of behaviour, we were able to identify the emotional energy that was driving the reactive behaviour and deactivate it.

What I love about Matts relationship with his mom now is that, she's still the same, but their connection is quite different. Instead of taking everything she says as a personal attack and reacting to it, he is able to Let it Go!, water off a ducks back, sometime with a wee smile on his face as he remembers how it used to be!

Don't get me wrong, they still have their moments but these days Matt can use the trigger as a gift to release the next layer of incomplete emotional energy. Remember family will ALWAYS bring our biggest lessons. In most cases they come from the same patterns of conditioning as us and have developed strategies and coping mechanisms of their own that are deeply connected to those you created for yourself.

Before I came across Becs and her coaching, I was at the whim of my emotions. I had NO idea we have the ability to control our emotions by simply feeling them out instead f letting them control us, and just wallowing in how we for hours, days, months, or years!

Now, after having worked with her, I know that NO MATTER what I am feeling or how I react initially to something, I have the power to process whatever it is I am feeling and be able to get myself grounded and be PRESENT in the moment which then allows me to tackle the situation at hand.

Matt Dillingham – Founder of In The Black

LOOKING FOR LOVE

I started working with a private client, who I knew had had an extremely challenging childhood. Filled with physical, sexual and emotional abuse, she had spent her life looking for acceptance, love and happiness from others, believing she must be unlovable.

Ashley had searched for love and acceptance in all the wrong places, believing there must be something out there that would make her feel better. Maybe someone who would love her. She turned to alcohol and recreational drugs early in life, as a way to *Avoid the Present*, where the emotional pain lives.

She found herself in relationships that didn't serve her. Men who abused and beat her, but for her this was normal, it somehow felt familiar and after all it was what she had been told and experienced and therefore it was all she believed she deserved.

Lurking deep inside our coding is this pervasive feeling that something is missing! It is this very **Human Control Code** that the personal development empire is built upon, people looking for the answer to this question;

When I get........(new car, married, a promotion at work, more money, more love) I will be Happy.

Consider this.

The moment your umbilical cord is cut and you are born into the world, all the needs you had previously had been met automatically, therefore it just felt like mum was a part of you, but now you have complete dependence on others to meet those needs to keep you alive. To feed you, comfort you, protect you and make you feel happy and because you don't yet have language to interpret what is happening to you, a feeling level decision is made that a part of me must be missing and it's the part of me that meets my needs and makes me feel safe.

So, we go on a lifelong quest in search of the thing that is missing that will make us feel whole and complete again.

We chase after goals and desires or that special someone to love us with an undercurrent of hope that this will be the thing that finally makes us happy or fulfils us. The problem is that no amount of love, attention, money, time, possessions, experiences, accomplishments, that can possibly make us feel whole and complete, because there was nothing missing in the first place.

There is actually nothing that can satisfy this longing for a sense of completion, but we keep trying thinking that the next thing will finally do it for us.

One of the aspects of the **Human Control Codes** is what we refer to as *Mistaking Need for Love*. We search for that feeling of completion from other people and expect them to fulfil and meet our needs and to LOVE us!

Seeking Validation.

Love is essentially a state of being, not something that you give or get from others.

After our second session, during which Ashley released a number of energies from deep inside. Just by allowing herself to be present to them, allowing herself for the first time ever to sit and allow the energy of the incomplete emotional experience to be felt fully, until there was nothing left to feel.

As she released the energy she found that she was able to detach herself emotionally from what she had experienced and from this space she wrote this piece of poetry;

Sitting up on your throne you think you got away with murder,

What? Really you think I would not remember.

The hurt, the pain, the way you made me feel,

The anger, the loss of control, total fits of despair.

You took something from me I can never get back,

My innocence, my childhood I grew up way to fast.

You left me broken, trashed inside and out,

You left me lying in the shadows of darkness and doubt.

So many times, I lost hope and felt I couldn't go on,

Like my rainbows were now just puddles of melted crayon.

Often, I felt ugly, worthless, like the world would be better off,

If I were no longer here, just to let you win and scoff.

The pain got too much I couldn't take any more, I took a blade to my wrist and watched

the blood trickle to the floor,

You stole my smile, you stole my laughter,

What remained was a really good actor.

For I kept your secret for long enough,

I blocked it out the only way I knew how.

That secret tore me down and destroyed my soul,

It was the beginning of my nightmares, a show on the road.

I believed for so long what you did was some kind of normal,

It took me a long time to realise, your lack of judgement, and character was immoral.

I let so many others do the same to me,

As I felt that was all I was worth, why couldn't you see.

I have fought for so long to survive, I am just tired and broken,

But the only way from here, is up and out into the open.

I am no longer that little girl drowning in a pool of fear,

Because I am now a mother, a protector with a voice so beware!

While we continue to work together, Ashley is one of the most inspirational clients I have ever worked with, not only is she addressing her emotional, physical and sexual abuse she also made the decision to give up alcohol and cigarettes which were her default escape mechanisms.

10 weeks ago, I got to the point where things were getting too much, the stress and pressures of life, and I continued to internalise it all, and it was just complete and utter chaos. Externally my life was just as bad. I was drinking every night, smoking more and barley sleeping. I was trying to block out the feelings and emotions inside and not deal with what was happening for me.

Since I was six years old I had developed some pretty strong coping mechanisms, and built on them over the years, as I allowed myself to become a victim to multiple perpetrators, and experiences. I got to a point where I could no longer see any light, I felt like I had to constantly put on a mask to please everyone, but I really wanted out, I didn't want to go on.

I knew this was my last chance, and I was so very grateful to have been given the opportunity to start working with Rebecca. When I first met with her, there was something calming about her, and for someone who had worked with many professionals over the years, this was the first time I had felt that, she came across in a non-threatening manner, and I was able to relax.

Since I began working with Rebecca 10 weeks ago, I have not had a drop of alcohol, I haven't had a cigarette in 8 weeks, and just recently I have been able to sleep more than 7 hours a night, 7 nights in a row, and that is just some of the physical achievements.

For someone that has experienced 23 years of abuse, in different forms I had developed some extremely unhealthy coping mechanisms to allow myself to deal with what was happening to me, but not feeling the emotional energies attached to the physical aspects. I became easily triggered by different situations and some people described it like they felt they had to walk on egg shells around me, scared they would say something wrong.

Working together with Rebecca, we have managed to break a fair amount of the coping mechanisms I had developed, and she has taught me how to process the emotional energies, feeling them fully and letting them go in a safe and supportive environment, rather than holding onto them.

Having someone that committed to helping me was completely foreign territory, and it took me a while to realize that she wasn't going anywhere, even if I wanted to, she wasn't going to back down and walk away.
Together I have been able to face many of my demons and learned to trust more, and open up.

I now realise that my external chaos was reflecting what was happening on the inside, and that the emotions were driving my behaviours.

When Rebecca and I finally got to the bottom of what was holding kw back, and trapping me in this chaos, I felt a huge shift of energy, and for the first time ever in my life I finally felt inner peace, and it has been amazing. I have been able to sleep all night, I have felt so much better within myself, my external world including my daughter has calmed down dramatically, and situations I never thought I would be able to handle without being triggered, I have been able to breeze through.

The tools Rebecca has taught me are the most valuable ones I will ever learn in my life and will stay with me now forever. I feel so much positivity about what the future holds, my perspectives are changing, and I can see things much clearer.

I could not have done this without the support and teachings Rebecca has brought into my life, and they will not only continue to benefit me, but each and every whanau I work with every day. Empowerment Is an amazing thing, and that is exactly what Rebecca has helped me achieve.

We become stuck inside patterns of behaviour, patterns that define who we are and they are what we call our *Identity Codes*. We try to control our environments to keep us away from the fear and the pain and the resulting emotional overwhelm. We become stuck in our ways, comfortable in the roles we play. They become our self-definition, a good girl, not very clever, always sick, the black sheep of the family, not loveable, stubborn.

We all want to have a stable, secure and safe foundation for our lives. As such, we like to have things that we can depend upon, things that don't change. However, there isn't anything in creation that isn't changing even if the changes are sometimes imperceptible.

Sometimes we become deeply identified with old emotional pain it somehow feels familiar to have it there. We get a feeling of security that we can depend on it always being there, it has become part of who you identify yourself with and if you were to let it go, there is a feeling you would lose an essential part of who you are.

In fact, anything that has been around for a long time can become a source of identification; your job or career, your name, your status or degree, your body, your reputation, your home, spouse or children, your habits and conditioning, your ideology or beliefs or religion.

But none of these are things are truly non-changing. These things are all subject to change but we **Resist Change** in an attempt to protect our sense of self.

THE ANGRIEST BOY I HAVE EVER MET!

Josh's Dad was registered blind, his sight had deteriorated consistently over a 20 year period because of a hereditary condition. Joshs' mum had left the family home when he was 10 years old and Josh lived with his Dad and sister in a small town in rural New Zealand. An incident at school saw Josh being stood down from the school for aggressive behaviour. It wasn't long before this type of behaviour became a regular occurrence so that by the time I was called in, Josh was 14 years old and the school and police were at a loss as to what to do next.

Excluded from the local schools and suspended from an Alternative Education program, Joshs' future was looking very bleak indeed, saved only from a criminal conviction by his under 16 status.

Josh was probably the angriest child I had ever met. He sat arms folded scowling at me from the other side of a table in a small room located at the Ministry of Education offices, I had refused to see Josh at my private clinic after I had seen his file.

His knuckles were grazed and he was very tense and he just glowered at me, tight lipped.

I looked at him and spelled it out;

"I am it! I am your last Hope. If you don't take this opportunity, you are going to be in a box with bars or a box with a lid. I am going to teach you two very simple tools that will help you process the emotional energy that you have built up inside."
He looked at me from under his baseball cap and said with tears in his eyes;

"I don't have feelings!"

As his story unfolded it became more and more obvious to me how scared this kid was. The aggression was just a defence mechanism and because of Joshs' earlier behaviour and school exclusions he and his dad and sister had moved into town, the rough end. Because of his posturing and Bulletproof attitude Josh had become a target for members of a local gang. He was always on edge, always ready to fight, always ready to defend his dad who had also become an easy target. He had been caught up in a situation that was gaining momentum and was running out of control. He was so scared, but didn't know what else to do other than to aggressively defend himself and his family.

This aggressive behaviour had been directed towards those trying to help him and a situation with a police officer had brought him to the edge and into my program.

Josh and I met twice a week for a 6 week period and as our rapport and his trust in me grew he was able to open up allowing me to teach him how to access and deactivate the emotional energy that was running the show.

He relaxed, his behaviour at home became calm and laid back. The family caught another lucky break and were rehoused into a different area of town. A change in environment and the support that the family were receiving from the government agencies was providing Josh with hope and new focus.
Josh had made such great progress in such a short period of time, I wanted to test his resolve. I wanted to put him into a pressured situation and see what reaction was triggered. I invited the police officer that Josh had had an altercation with to come and meet with Josh to talk through the situation and to give Josh the opportunity to apologise.

When I told Josh what was planned, the reactive energy that came up was intense. He became verbally aggressive and agitated, telling me I'd double crossed him and he would just punch the officer if he came into the room. Perfect opportunity for Josh to Deactivate the emotional energy that was coursing through his body! Slowly but surely as the energy dissipated Josh calmed, he sat in his seat arms folded tightly across his chest, scowling at me;

"I'll just run" he kept repeating, *"I'll just run."*

I took him through a process and got Josh to simply just sit with the energy and to feel it as it came up. (It was also a great opportunity for me to resolve some energy also, as it was like being inside a pressure cooker.)

The door opened and you could have cut the atmosphere with a knife. Josh stayed in his seat and allowed the officer to speak. When it came to his turn Josh lifted his eyes, look at him squarely and said, I am sorry! Some playful banter was exchanged and there was an open and frank conversation around choices. For Josh it was a very positive experience and at the end of the meeting they both stood up, shook hands and then hugged.

Three weeks later it was agreed that Josh would be allowed to return to the Alternative Education Program, where he has been a model student and a return to main stream schooling is being considered for next year.

The oldest and youngest foodbank volunteers, Maureen Paterson and Josh Stannard. Photo/Andrew Warner.

PLAYING LIFE SAFE

One of the areas that I found myself struggling with during the process of writing this book was what New Zealanders call *Tall Poppy Syndrome*. It is born from the fear of social isolation and loneliness and it is coded into our conditioning in the form of **holding back** or **Playing it Safe**.

When you are little and you have the experience of others withdraw from you, revoking their love and support, teasing and taunting you, it can cause such a deep emotional pain that it has us toeing the line, not wishing to upset others or express ourselves for fear of ridicule.

It is the number one tool in the Parental Emotional Manipulation Tool Kit and the number one driver in the People Pleaser.

It is reinforced further when we experience being criticised or made fun of whenever we have attempted to be powerfully self-expressed or display our individuality.

We develop a sense of who we are from the feeling of being connected to our friends and family and let's face it most of these people are not particularly powerfully self-expressed in the world, in fact very few people are. We develop a habit of holding ourselves back from being fully self-expressed and unknowingly participate in a game that we call –Let's all stay ordinary together! Because we are looking for the sense of connection from those around us and having them like us, accept us, or approve of us it is something that we can't afford to be without. We feel that they may pull away from us if we express ourselves differently, so in fear we end up playing the small me.

We are also afraid that even people who don't know us will disapprove of us or our creative expression. We're afraid that people will hate on us and talk negatively about us behind our backs. Strangely enough our powerful self-expression in the world is something people don't want to see because it reminds them that they are not living up to their own true potential.

We also have a fear that we will be lonely and alone because those around us, friends and family will pull away from us if we are truly successful.

The reality however is that when you are powerfully self- expressed you just hang out with new friends who are also being powerfully self-expressed.

Being powerfully self-expressed should not be confused with being emotionally aggressive, manipulative, coercive, angry or belligerent. That's not at all what is meant by powerful self-expression. What remains after the coding has been deactivated is confidence, self-empowerment and a feeling of being grounded. Individuals who feel connected and comfortable in their own skin are not afraid to be who they are here to be.

OUT OF CONTROL

Cara was like a lot of my clients and came because she was worried about her sons' behaviour. Noah was displaying anxiety and isolating himself and more recently and concerning was the aggressive behaviour he was displaying at school. He had developed an elaborate night time ritual and was developing other behaviours that were concerning her.

Noah had developed patterns of behaviour that prevented him from having to interact with the other children at school. He would spend a lot of time alone, choosing to sit on the perimeter of groups and play by himself at recess. Cara felt he was isolated and separate from his peer group and he had a need to control his environment to make him feel safe. This was becoming difficult for him and when he couldn't control his friends' behaviours it caused frustration and this had resulted in aggressive out bursts at school, which pushed his peer group further away causing further frustration and isolation. His night time routine involed praying for everyone in the family and friends, individualy.

His mum was distraught. She brought him to his first session, she stayed as I explained the method and then I asked her to leave. Mum leaving was enough of a trigger for me to teach Noah one of the techniques, he was very quick to pick up it up and was able to experience the emotional release when he deactivated the energy source. As he did, his need to control his world diminished, he was able to process the emotions as they arose, preventing the build-up (frustration) and release (aggressive behaviour). The night time ritual stopped and although choosing not to involve himself fully, group activities were no longer causing the huge anxiety they had done in the past. Noah discovered Cross fit and at 13 is training 6 days a week with a goal to be in the Youth Cross Fit Games next year.

After the almost instant result Cara observed her son achieve, she joined my **Feeling Level Bootcamp** and realised very quickly that she too had some limiting behaviours and ways of being and it was in fact her who had taught her boy to behave the way he had been behaving!

Cara had experienced a massive emotional trauma when she was 15 years old. Three of her closest friends had been killed in a car accident and this traumatic experience had activated behaviour patterns in Cara that meant she had become very controlling of her environment. She had developed these behaviours as a way to ensure that the people she loved and cared for were kept safe.

What the trauma had done was create stress for herself and anxiety in her son. She had modelled to him that he needed to control his own environment to ensure he did not have to experience the emotional overwhelm she had been trying to avoid. She had taught him to be anxious.

My life before I started this process was simply put.... not lived but just living. I had a son who was experiencing anxiety, stress and wanted to control outcomes. What I didn't realise until I was sitting in that chair with Rebecca was that I was conditioning him to be this way through my everyday behaviours. He was only demonstrating behaviours learned from me.
Using the Human Control Codes as a guide I had to truly face up to what kind of world I lived in and therefore by default my son lived in. Through childhood experiences or preconditioning from my own mother, passed down from her mother I realised that I wasn't truly living... I was existing.

My son was a reflection of me and my experience. Here I was afraid of the universe, what it could dish out at me that I would try and control my environments by being absolutely prepared for every situation. By being brutally honest with everyone including my son - because he needed to know that life wasn't fluffy ducks - just in case. My son would witness me not overreact to situation or avoid emotional situations.

What did that mean for my son?

That meant that he too couldn't cope without the control. He too didn't feel things fully - always approach with caution. He would avoid anything that was new or unknown with huge amounts of fear and anxiety. He would work to everyones' expectations, not dare to push the limits in activities, school or home.

Using the Becs' process I have been able to see clearly the world I had created around me. I held onto those fears with such force that I was afraid to really live. My world was limited greatly - even through prior to sitting in that chair I would have tried to convince you that I had it sorted.

When the clouds lifted, truly lifted I could see clearly! My world isn't controlled by fear. I can be my true self! I am completely present!

My son has grown so much since I started working on myself! He has gone from being so shy he couldn't order food from Subway to just recently performing on stage in front of 1000 people! He felt so proud and can't wait until the next opportunity!

When we try and control our environment, or we ***Try to Force an Outcome*** it is in response to the fear of not being taken care of and not kept safe. These traumas have become self-defining and have become part of your **EGO**, your sense of self, of who you are!

The trauma of being separated from your mother at birth and many other traumatic experiences associated with becoming an individual human being can be just too emotionally overwhelming for us.

This **Human Control Code** is one of the most insidious. This **Central Control Code** is the result of being conditioned to feel that we are our EGO.

It becomes coded into us just from growing up in an environment where everyone feels that they are the collection of their life stories, accomplishments, disappointments, traumas, pleasures and all their other experiences.

This modelling seeps into us by osmosis. After all, if everyone is going around believing that they are the collection of their life experiences there isn't really any other frame of reference available from which to learn.

The consequence of this conditioning is that we feel like an isolated individual, we feel separate from and at odds with the world around us. This isolation causes us to feel that if something is going to happen then I better make it happen.

If it is to be it is upto me. This is the powerful voice of this code of conditioning.

Have you ever had the experience of having a desire and then forgetting about it, only to have the desire fulfilled without seeming to have had to take any action at all?

This is because in reality, the laws of nature are doing everything even when it seems that our body, mind and personality are involved in the process.

It is only our identification with our body, mind, personality, thoughts and actions that causes us to believe that we are an individual.

Your essential nature isn't your body, your mind, your thoughts, your experiences, your personality, your opinions. You are limitless pure potential to be and experience anything.

Think for a moment about the experience referred to as being in the *zone*. This concept is frequently talked about in the world of sports. When someone is playing in the zone, time slows down, everything is effortless, it seems almost like you are not doing it (and you're not by the way). It's happening through you. That's being in sync with the universe and the laws of nature.

The universe operates on a law called *The Law of Least Action* or *The Law of Least Effort*. The planets travel around the sun in a path of least effort, an ellipse, not a square or rectangle. This law of least effort is what orchestrates plants to grow and babies to develop inside the womb. It is the law that causes electrons to spin around the nucleus of an atom in the simplest of paths. It governs the rise and fall of the tides the sun and the moon and every other natural process.

Everything in nature happens with least effort and in perfect timing. This includes everything that happens to us as well.

However, our conditioning of thinking and feeling that we are an isolated individual, who is creating our reality, causes us to Force and Struggle and Suffer whilst trying to *make it happen* MY WAY and IN MY TIMING! Forcing things to happen your way or in your timing may result in superficially seeming to get what it is that you think you want.

It is our identification with our EGO that causes us to force life into showing up the way that we want it to. When we think and feel that we are separate from the rest of the universe, that we are isolated and alone then we really can't help but try to make things happen the way that we think they should.

However, our inability to sense the natural timing of things, our over-riding urge to try to control how things happen causes us to attempt to **Force Outcomes**.

What is needed is to learn to relax and allow life to show up in its own perfection and natural effortless timing. However, this is something that we are deeply conditioned not to do. Thus, we struggle and suffer needlessly because we are out of sync with the law of least effort.

THE NEED TO BE RIGHT

We are very attached to our EGO, it defines our sense of self. When our way of seeing things (our perspective) is threatened or our way of seeing the world is challenged or violated we tend to **Exclude Other Perspectives**.

This **Human Control Code** is where bigotry and prejudice live. It is the source of most disagreements, fighting and wars in the world and in our homes.

It is expressed in all forms of fundamentalism, and is the real basis of religious wars, ethnic and racial discrimination, and much of our inability to get along with each other collectively as well as in individual relationships and families.

When you become identified with your perspective, your particular beliefs become part of your self-definition.

These self-definitions are really not who you are. But they are so compelling that they really feel like they are a part of us. This makes you very vulnerable to having your sense of self threatened if you allow yourself to be open to seeing things in a new or different way, so you avoid that.

Your way becomes the only way, not only for you but for everyone else too. My way or the highway!

You can't afford to be open to another way of seeing things as it is too much of a threat to your very sense of your existence. So, you stay closed minded and isolated, feeling that you are right and how can all these other stupid people in the world not see things like you do.

We become very attached and enmeshed in our stories about the past and become very attached to our expectations of how things SHOULD be. We spend a lot of time and energy projecting possible negative outcomes onto the future which cause us anxiety and we end up reacting often excessively when things don't go the way we thought and imagined they should.

We Bias our Reality.

We all know people who have been adversely affected in the past and they just can't seem to get over it. The event is long gone but the stories about the event live on in the mind of the person so much so that they are living inside of their story and cannot be fully present.

Some people live in a story about how things will be in the future, either Rainbows and Unicorns or Doom and Gloom. Whether the story is about the past or the future it absorbs our attention and it occupies our minds and it seems like the story is a part of who we are.

Attempting to make meaning of our experiences is a very human thing to do. But when we become identified with the stories that we make up about our experiences and live in these stories as if the events were still impinging upon our life we are then no longer present to the reality of what is.
Most people spend so much of their time trying to understand and make sense of their experiences that they rarely live in the present moment.

This conditioning is an identification with our thinking and intellect. The conditioning will dominate your experience and you'll tend to be caught up in the stories until you learn how to experientially extract your awareness from being identified with the story.

The only place the story exists is inside your head. Stories about what may or may not happen in the future play out as anxiety and stories of the past tend to cause us to be depressed as we focus on the bad stuff that happened.

Whenever we are caught up in an expectation we are living in the illusion that the universe will organize life to be the way that we want it to be. When it doesn't we tend to over-react with anger, disappointment and frustration. This over-reaction keeps us absorbed inside of the energy of our emotional reaction. We stay identified with the expectation, the story out of which the expectation has been made and to our 'legitimate' emotional reaction.

TWO FACED TESSA

Tessa is one of the sweetest, friendliest, happiest individuals you will ever meet. Despite her circumstances she is always positive and upbeat, a real joy to be around.

I was delivering my programme through a local charitable Trust, who provide emergency housing and support for families in crisis. I had been asked to deliver my programme to a group of 6 women over a 3-month period.

The intention of the programme was to teach the girls my method for Identifying and Deactivating their conditioned and learnt behaviour.

The results the Trust were looking for were, more engagement from the ladies, an increase in personal responsibility, a willingness to address addictive behaviours and a commitment to moving forward in securing themselves private housing and an income source.

Tessa and her two children were one of the families I was working with. She had heard the presentation I had given to the organisation and was first in line for an individual session. She quickly identified a pattern of behaviour and was able to access the energy of the feeling, she released the energy, and sparkled even brighter after our session, she came to two further sessions and seemed to really enjoy them and then she stopped coming.

Whenever I asked if anyone had seen or heard from Tessa, the response was always the same.
"She's good, happy as always."

But she was clearly avoiding me and not coming to programme.

This is a pattern I have observed with almost all my adult clients. The avoidance strategy.

We create all sorts of excuses as to why we can't or don't need to come to sessions, usually when we need the support the most.

We all hold a huge amount of Fear around how we look to others and allowing ourselves to be completely vulnerable takes a lot of courage.

The role of a coach is to hold you accountable, to provoke you into indentifying your patterns of behaviour, in a safe space.

No one can help you if you don't turn up to session and do the work!

Programme became compulsory and subject to consequences and Tessa came back to session.

We sat together and completed **The Happy Set Point** assessment (available at www.becsmcewan.com)

Tessa scored really highly. She relaxed and chatted openly as we went through the questions, she was happy and upbeat as always.

"I have been using your techniques and they really work, I have removed lots of energies and life is going really well.'

When we finished the assessment I introduced her to kinesiology and we re-asked the questions this time we bypassed her conditioning and thought process and asked her body and nervous system the questions using muscel testing.

After scoring very low on the first 5 questions she burst into tears as the mask was stripped away and she saw what lay behind it. Her reality and her truth were uncovered.

She had managed to convinced herself and those around her she was happy but the reality was she was miserable, out of control and wanted the world to stop and let her off!

When she glimpsed behind the mask she saw that her behaviour was just a coping mechanism she had developed to escape and hide from the emotional pain she was in.

Most other methods and service providers teach you further coping mechanisms, ways to manage control or escape from the internal pressure.

I help you to Identify and Deactivate the source code and the pattern of behaviour falls away. It is a very simple and a very effective way to deal with all behaviours.

If you believe that you must learn to live with your anxiety or watch your child suffer and there is nothing that can be done, it's just the way you are! Or perhaps it runs in the family or maybe you believe that medication is the only option! I am here to share with you to tell you that the only reason you experience anxiety is because you haven't learned to effectively resolve intense emotions or traumas. It's as simple as learning to do the exact opposite of what you have been taught and conditioned to do!

Becs has given me tools to use and I have found them very useful to lift a down and heavy mood and let it go so I feel light and free from the stress these moods carry with them.

I find myself in a different frame of mind and able, when ready to deal with whatever it may be in a totally different way, a whole new approach can make such a huge difference. Each time I am blessed to meet with Becs the more I learn and the more I recognise the behaviour patterns I run. Becoming engulfed in bad moods, feeling let down or overwhelmed by the situation.

Each time we meet the stronger and more in control I feel with my emotional state. I can choose to let it suffocate me or I can use the tools I have been taught to rise above all the chaos and let it go.

Janine (Te Tuinga Whanau - Client)

Never in my wildest dreams did I imagine that one decision could impact my life in such a profound way. March 1999, I found out I was pregnant with baby number 3, my daughter was two and my son 5 months old, I made the devastating decision to terminate the baby thinking ad no other choice at the time.

I was left traumatised by the whole experience and felt like a part of me died that day too, then two years later I found myself getting divorced and started my journey as a single mum.

It was challenging mentally and emotionally and physically but I kept soldering on thinking this was my life now and I deserved everything because I had taken my babies life.

15 years later I was introduced to the concept that we have useful and not useful emotions and how we have incomplete experiences that can make us feel extremely uncomfortable.

As I learned more and practiced what I was taught I completely forgave myself and realised that nothing in my life was ng because of that decision I had just stopped living my life fully.

To this day I use the techniques not only on myself but with my family, friends and community.

My life has totally transformed I will be eternally grateful for being blessed with being set free. Free to be me.

Tracy Hamilton – Founder at Pure Heart Leadership

In Summary

Throughout the book I mention the **Human Control Codes**. Whilst working with my clients I noticed 12 reccuring patterns of behavior they all had in common these are what I now refer to as the **Human Control Codes**, they are in no particular order:

- Resisting Feeling Things Fully / Limiting Possibities
- Ignoring Your Instincts
- Being Judgemental
- Getting Distracted / Avoiding the Present
- Compromising Your Integrity
- Seeking Validation / Mistaking Need for Love
- Fearing or Resisting Change
- Playing it Safe / Limiting Self Expression
- Trying to Force an Outcome
- Needing to be Right
- Manufacturing Interpretations / Making up Shit
- Over-Reacting

My experience is we all run these patterns of behavior and until the energy has been Deactivated in each and every one they will continue to run our lives subconsciously.

If you would like further information on the Human Control Codes or would like to experience a session with me please go to my website at: www.becsmcewan.com where you will find a link to my calander.

HIRE BECS TO SPEAK AT YOUR EVENT!

Book Becs McEwan as your Keynote Speaker and You're Guaranteed to Make Your Event Highly Entertaining and Unforgettable!

For over a decade, Becs McEwan has been educating, and helping parents, children and families understand the direct link between Feelings and Behaviour. Sharing with them her proven method for Identifying and Deactivating the underlying cause of Difficult Behaviour and techniques to Eliminate the patterns that have parents questioning why they decided to have children in the first place.

Her origin story includes a near death experience after an eating disorder took control, her own struggle with depression, anxiety and deep-seated anger that had her lashing out at those she loved with verbal aggression. Her addiction to nicotine and the precscribed pharmaceutical anti-depressent meds. After successfully curing herself from what she calls Adult Bad Behaviour, Becs can share relevant, actionable strategies that anyone can use - even if they have tried everything before and nothing has worked.

Her unique style inspires, empowers and entertains audiences while giving them the tools and strategies they need and want to help their child and regain some peace and calm in the warzone that the family home has become.

For more info, visit www.becsmcewan.com

ONE LAST THING...

If you enjoyed this book or found it useful I'd be very grateful if you'd post a short review on Amazon. Your support really does make a difference and I read all the reviews personally so I can get your feedback and make this book even better.

I

Thanks again for your support!

Printed in Australia
AUHW012225250319
310277AU00004B/11

9 781642 556919